Cocktails

Classic & contemporary drinks to mix

PENGUIN BOOKS

Penguin Group (Australia)
250 Camberwell Road, Camberwell, Victoria 3124, Australia
Penguin Books Ltd
80 Strand, London WC2R 0RL, England
Penguin Group (NZ)
67 Apollo Drive, Mairangi Bay, Auckland 1310, New Zealand

First published by Penguin Group (Australia), a division of Pearson Australia Group Pty Ltd, 2004

3 5 7 9 10 8 6 4 2

This collection copyright © Penguin Group (Australia) 2004

All rights reserved. Without limiting the rights under copyright reserved above, no part of this publication may be reproduced, stored in or introduced into a retrieval system, or transmitted, in any form or by any means (electronic, mechanical, photocopying, recording or otherwise), without the prior written permission of both the copyright owner and the above publisher of this book.

Design by Karen Trump © Penguin Group (Australia)
Illustrations by Pat Kermode/Purple Rabbit Productions
Cover photograph by Brian Hagiwara/Getty Images
Typeset in 10/13 pt Frutiger by Midland Typesetters, Maryborough, Victoria
Printed and bound in Australia by McPherson's Printing Group, Maryborough, Victoria

National Library of Australia
Cataloguing-in-Publication data:

Cocktails: classic & contemporary drinks to mix.

ISBN-13: 978 0 14 300255 0.
ISBN-10: 0 14 300255 4.

1. Cocktails.

641.874

www.penguin.com.au

COCKTAIL

Originally defined as a short, dry aperitif, but now refers to any of various short mixed drinks. Sometimes exotically coloured, often shaken, usually chilled, frequently sweetened. Their history is long with exact origin unknown.

Having a party? Want to mix an elegant drink to impress? Relaxing by the pool? Or curling up by the fire? In *Cocktails* you'll find a classic, tropical or original recipe to suit every occasion. Have fun with some of today's most fashionable mixed drinks. You may even be inspired to create your own personal cocktail!

Contents

How to use this book	vii
Brandy	1
Gin	13
Liqueur	24
Rum	40
Tequila	54
Vodka	64
Whisky	78
Wine	88
Punch	98
Non-alcoholic	109
Hot toddy	118
Morning after	130
Glasses	136
Glossary	139

How to use this book

Recipes are listed by their base spirit (brandy, tequila, etc) or type (punch, non-alcoholic, etc). Please see the glossary for an explanation of ingredients and terms.

It is crucial that a cocktail looks attractive, and that means using the correct glass. Each recipe suggests which glass to use, and the various types are described at the back of the book.

For most recipes, you will require a cocktail shaker, an electric blender or simply a long-handled barspoon for stirring. You will also require plenty of ice (either cubes or crushed).

All recipes are for 1 serving, unless otherwise specified.

BRANDY

From the Dutch BRANDEWIJN *(burnt wine). A generic term for any spirit distilled from fermented fruit juice. The honey-coloured spirit made from grapes is the most common brandy.*

Bengal

45 ml brandy
15 ml maraschino
15 ml triple sec
30 ml pineapple juice
2 dashes of angostura bitters

Half-fill a shaker with ice cubes, pour in all ingredients and shake well. Strain into a cocktail glass.

Between the Sheets

30 ml Cointreau
30 ml brandy
30 ml white rum
15 ml lemon juice
lemon peel

Shake first four ingredients with ice. Strain into a champagne saucer and add a twist of lemon.

Bosom Caresser

15 ml madeira
7 ml brandy
7 ml orange curaçao
5 ml grenadine
1 egg yolk

In a mixing glass half-filled with crushed ice, combine all ingredients. Stir well. Strain into a cocktail glass.

Brandy Alexander

60 ml brandy
30 ml crème de cacao
30 ml pouring cream
freshly grated nutmeg

Shake first three ingredients with ice.
Strain into a cocktail glass and sprinkle
lightly with nutmeg.

Claret is the liquor for boys; port for men; but he who aspires to be a hero must drink brandy.

— SAMUEL JOHNSON

Brantini

45 ml brandy
30 ml gin
splash of dry vermouth
lemon peel

Stir first three ingredients with crushed ice and strain into an old-fashioned glass over ice cubes. Add a twist of lemon.

Grapefruit Nog

45 ml brandy
½ cup grapefruit juice
30 ml lemon juice
1 tablespoon honey
1 egg

Whiz all ingredients in a blender, with ½ cup crushed ice, briefly and at low speed. Pour into a Collins glass over ice cubes.

Horse's Neck

lemon peel
ginger ale
60 ml whisky

Drape end of lemon peel over the edge of a Collins glass. Fill with ice cubes. Add whisky and fill with ginger ale. Stir well.

Scorpion

lime wedge
30 ml white rum
30 ml dark rum
30 ml brandy
30 ml orgeat
30 ml orange juice
30 ml lime juice
2 dashes of sugar syrup
strawberry or pineapple spear
fresh mint sprig

Fill a 250 ml wine glass with ice, add lime wedge and transfer into shaker. Add remaining ingredients (except strawberry/pineapple and mint), shake and pour back into glass. Garnish with strawberry or pineapple, and mint. Serve with a straw.

Mikado

30 ml brandy
dash of triple sec
dash of grenadine
dash of crème de noyeaux
dash of angostura bitters

Pour all ingredients over ice cubes in an old-fashioned glass and stir.

GIN

From the French GENÉVRIER *(juniper).
A dry, colourless spirit originally
made from juniper berries, but now
distilled from grain. Until the Gin Act
of 1736, gin was sold cheaper than
beer in London.*

Alaska

60 ml London dry gin
15 ml (or less) green Chartreuse
lemon peel
extra spiral of lemon peel

Stir gin and Chartreuse in a mixing
glass with crushed ice, then strain into
a cocktail glass and add a twist of lemon.
Drape lemon peel spiral over the glass
rim.

Alice Springs

20 ml lemon juice
20 ml orange juice
½ teaspoon grenadine
3 drops angostura bitters
60 ml gin
soda water
½ orange slice

Combine lemon juice, orange juice, grenadine, angostura bitters and gin in a shaker with 5 ice cubes, and shake. Pour into a highball glass, fill with soda and sit orange slice on rim.

Clover Club

45 ml gin
40 ml lime juice
40 ml grenadine
1 egg white
spiral of lime peel

Shake first four ingredients with ice. Strain into a frosty cold cocktail glass. Drape lime peel over the glass rim.

Gimlet

45 ml gin
10 ml lime cordial
spiral of lemon peel

Shake gin and cordial with ice, strain into a chilled cocktail glass with a few ice cubes and drop the lime peel into the drink.

Gin and It

30 ml gin
30 ml sweet vermouth
orange slice

Pour the gin and vermouth into an old-fashioned glass. Add a few ice cubes and float orange slice in the drink.

Gin Sling

60 ml gin
15 ml cherry brandy
15 ml lemon juice
1 teaspoon castor sugar (optional)
soda water
slice of lemon and red maraschino cherry

Shake gin, brandy, juice and sugar well with ice. Strain into a Collins glass, add an ice cube and fill with soda. Form the lemon into a twisted ring on a toothpick with the cherry in the middle and balance across top of glass.

Candy
Is dandy
But liquor
Is quicker

— Ogden Nash

Classic (Dry) Martini

45 ml gin
5 ml dry vermouth
lemon peel
olive (optional)

Stir gin and vermouth with ice cubes in a mixing glass until just chilled. Quickly strain into a chilled cocktail glass. Add a twist of lemon and the olive (if you desire).

Sake

45 ml gin
15 ml sake
olive or lemon peel

Combine gin and sake in a mixing glass with crushed ice and stir well. Strain into a cocktail glass. Serve with olive or lemon twist.

Tom Collins

60 ml gin
45 ml lemon juice
7 ml sugar syrup
soda water
lemon peel (optional)

Combine gin, juice and sugar syrup in a tall highball glass. Stir well, add ice and fill with soda. Add a twist of lemon, if you wish.

LIQUEUR

*Any of a class of alcoholic
liqueurs, usually strong,
sweet and highly flavoured.*

Alabama Slammer

30 ml Southern Comfort
30 ml amaretto
15 ml sloe gin
dash of lemon juice

Pour first three ingredients over ice in a highball glass and stir. Add lemon juice. Alternatively, serve in a shot glass without ice.

Amaretto Sunrise

10 ml amaretto
120 ml orange juice
splash of grenadine

Mix together amaretto and orange juice. Pour into a cocktail glass and add grenadine to watch the sunrise!

Brown Cow

30 ml Kahlua
120 ml milk
freshly grated nutmeg

Fill a highball glass with ice, then pour in Kahlua and milk. Stir gently to mix and dust with nutmeg.

Caipiranha

2 teaspoons sugar
8 lime wedges
75 ml cachaça

Mix sugar and lime wedges in an old-fashioned glass. Fill glass with ice cubes. Pour cachaça into glass and stir well.

Chocolate Cake

15 ml Malibu
15 ml dark crème de cacao
dash of cream
dash of Frangelico

Shake all ingredients with ice and strain into a liqueur glass.

Grasshopper

30 ml green crème de menthe
30 ml white crème de cacao
30 ml pouring cream
red and green maraschino cherries

Shake first three ingredients well with ice. Strain into a frosty cold cocktail glass. Spear red and green cherries alternately on a toothpick and place across top of glass.

Jellyfish

15 ml white crème de cacao
15 ml amaretto
Bailey's Irish Cream
grenadine

Pour crème de cacao and amaretto into a shot glass. Float enough Irish Cream on top to cover, and finally add a few drops of grenadine to create your jellyfish. Do not stir.

Pousse-Café

10 ml grenadine
10 ml maraschino
10 ml green crème de menthe
10 ml crème de violette
10 ml green Chartreuse
10 ml brandy or cognac

Carefully pour liqueurs over the back of a spoon into a pousse-café glass, in the order above, to create a layered drink. *Do not stir.*

Sauzaliky

½ banana
30 ml tequila
splash of orange juice
dash of lemon juice

Break banana into chunks and combine with other ingredients in blender. Whiz with crushed ice and serve in a highball glass.

It is only the first bottle that is expensive.

—FRENCH PROVERB

Sidecar

60 ml brandy or cognac
7 ml Cointreau
7 ml lemon juice
spiral of lemon peel

Shake first three ingredients well with ice and strain into a cocktail glass. Drop lemon peel in drink.

Note: For a Boston Sidecar, add 30 ml white rum.

Snowball

45 ml advocaat
90 ml lemonade
strawberry

Pour the advocaat into a large wine glass then slowly add the lemonade while stirring. Float the strawberry on top and serve with straws.

Watercolour

60 ml blue curaçao
60 ml peach schnapps
60 ml raspberry schnapps
pineapple juice
maraschino cherry or pineapple spear

Mix curaçao and schnapps together in a mixing glass and add pineapple juice to taste. Pour into a cocktail glass and garnish with cherry or pineapple.

RUM

A distillation of sugar cane or molasses, produced in a range of styles (and colours) from white to golden and dark, and varying considerably in flavour and potency.

Bahama Mama

dash of grenadine
45 ml dark rum
45 ml golden rum
45 ml white rum
60 ml sour mix
60 ml pineapple juice
75 ml orange juice
maraschino cherry and orange slice

Pour the grenadine into a Collins glass. Shake the next six ingredients well with crushed ice and strain into the glass. Garnish with cherry and orange slice.

Blue Chilli

60 ml blue curaçao
30 ml vodka
15 ml gin
15 ml white rum
dash of lemonade
lemon peel and maraschino cherry

Combine first four ingredients in a shaker with ice. Shake well and strain into a cocktail glass. Add lemonade. Garnish with lemon peel and cherry.

Brass Monkey

15 ml rum
15 ml vodka
120 ml orange juice

Combine rum and vodka in a shaker, stir gently. Pour in the orange juice and shake well. Serve over ice in a highball glass.

Daiquiri

45 ml white rum
30 ml lime juice
15 ml sugar syrup
lime peel

Shake first three ingredients with ice and strain into a cocktail glass or champagne saucer. Add a twist of lime.

Note: Some versions use egg white, which makes a frothier drink. For a drier version, omit the sugar syrup.

Hummer

30 ml coffee liqueur
30 ml white rum
2 scoops vanilla ice-cream

Whiz all ingredients, briefly, in blender at low speed. Pour into a highball glass.

Hurricane

30 ml white rum
30 ml dark rum
5 ml passionfruit syrup
15 ml lime juice

Shake all ingredients with ice and strain into a cocktail glass.

Jamaican Collins

75 ml dark rum
45 ml pineapple juice
1 teaspoon sugar
120 ml soda water

Half-fill a shaker with ice cubes. Pour in all ingredients except soda and shake well. Almost fill a highball glass with ice cubes and strain drink into glass. Add soda and stir well.

Jedi Mind Trick

30 ml dark rum
30 ml amaretto
30 ml Kahlua
30 ml Bailey's Irish Cream
3 scoops vanilla ice-cream
dash of pouring cream
2 maraschino cherries

Whiz all ingredients (except cherries) together in blender until smooth. Pour into a toddy glass and garnish with cherries.

If you were to ask me if I'd ever had the bad luck to miss my daily cocktail, I'd have to say that I doubt it; where certain things are concerned, I plan ahead.

– LUIS BUÑUEL

Lava Flow

1 banana
60 ml coconut cream
60 ml pineapple juice
30 ml white rum
30 ml Malibu
handful of strawberries

Blend banana, coconut cream and pineapple juice in blender and set aside. In a Collins glass, stir together rum, Malibu and strawberries. Pour banana mix into glass slowly. The rum and strawberries should creep up the sides of the glass.

Mai Tai

juice of one lime
30 ml white rum
30 ml dark rum
15 ml curaçao
15 ml orgeat or amaretto
pineapple spear, sliver of lime peel and fresh mint leaves

Half-fill a Collins glass with ice. Squeeze in lime juice, pour in the next four ingredients and stir. Slip the pineapple, lime sliver and mint onto a toothpick, balance across glass, and serve with straws.

Mojito

7 ml lime juice
1 teaspoon sugar
fresh mint leaves (plus an extra sprig)
60 ml white rum
soda water

Stir lime juice and sugar in a highball glass until sugar is dissolved. Crush mint leaves and rub along rim of glass, then discard. Add crushed ice and rum, stir well. Top up with soda and garnish with a fresh sprig of mint.

Pina Colada

60 ml white rum
30 ml coconut cream
120 ml pineapple juice
pineapple spear and maraschino cherry

Blend rum, coconut cream and juice with a scoop of crushed ice until smooth. Pour into a highball glass with ice cubes. Sit pineapple and cherry on rim of glass.

TEQUILA

A fiery Mexican spirit, distilled from the fermented agave plant. The colourless white or silver tequila is most common in Australia. By law, tequila must be produced from no less than 51% reducing sugars from the blue agave plant, with the remaining content from other natural sugars.

Acapulco

45 ml white rum
45 ml tequila
90 ml pineapple juice
90 ml grapefruit juice

Pour rum and tequila into an old-fashioned glass over ice. Top up with the juices.

Cactus Juice

45 ml tequila
30 ml amaretto
sour mix to fill

Build all ingredients in a Collins glass, over ice.

Lolita

20 ml tequila
10 ml lime juice
1 teaspoon honey
2 dashes of angostura bitters

Shake ingredients, strain into a cocktail glass and add a couple of ice cubes.

Long Island Iced Tea

15 ml tequila
15 ml vodka
15 ml white rum
15 ml gin
dash of cola
lemon or lime peel

Combine first four ingredients in a highball glass and stir gently. Add cola and garnish with lemon or lime twist.

Lumberjack

15 ml ouzo
15 ml sambuca
15 ml tequila
dash of Tabasco sauce

Pour first three ingredients into a shot glass. Add small dash of Tabasco sauce.

*I fear the man who drinks water
And so remembers what the rest of
us said last night.*

— ANCIENT GREEK SAYING

Margarita

lemon and salt
30 ml tequila
15 ml Cointreau or triple sec
10 ml lime or lemon juice

Frost the rim of a cocktail glass with lemon and salt. Shake remaining ingredients well with ice, then strain into the frosted glass.

Mexican Rose

20 ml tequila
10 ml strawberry schnapps
45 ml milk
15 ml grenadine

Shake ingredients together and strain into a shot glass.

Sloe Tequila

30 ml tequila
15 ml sloe gin
1 tablespoon lime juice
thin spiral of cucumber peel

Whiz first three ingredients in a blender, with ½ cup crushed ice, briefly and at low speed. Pour into an old-fashioned glass. Add ice cubes and spiral of cucumber peel.

VODKA

A refined, colourless spirit originally distilled from wheat, but now from corn, other cereals and potatoes. Vodka was being produced in Russia by the end of the ninth century, where distillers used fruit, herbs and spices to flavour their vodka because early production methods were crude.

After Sex

20 ml vodka
10 ml crème de banane
orange juice

Pour vodka and crème over some ice cubes in a Collins glass and fill with juice.

Apple Martini

20 ml vodka
20 ml apple schnapps
20 ml apple juice

Shake all ingredients well and strain into a cocktail glass.

Caipiroska

30 ml vodka
30 ml lime juice
½ teaspoon sugar

Shake all ingredients with ice and strain into a shot glass.

Mudslide

60 ml vodka
60 ml Kahlua
60 ml Bailey's Irish Cream

Combine ingredients with crushed ice in a shaker. Serve in a chilled highball glass.

Pink Panther

45 ml vodka
30 ml bourbon
30 ml coconut cream
30 ml pouring cream
10 ml grenadine
desiccated coconut and maraschino cherry

Combine first five ingredients in blender and whiz at low speed with crushed ice. Pour into a chilled wine glass. Dip cherry into coconut to coat, then place on rim of glass.

Some men are like musical glasses; to produce their finest tones you must keep them wet.

– SAMUEL TAYLOR COLERIDGE

Purple Hooter

15 ml crème de framboise
15 ml vodka
15 ml sour mix

Mix all ingredients together, chill with ice and strain into a shot glass. Shoot it!

Red Death

30 ml vodka
30 ml Southern Comfort
30 ml amaretto
15 ml sloe gin
15 ml triple sec
dash of lime juice
orange juice

Pour first six ingredients over ice in an old-fashioned glass. Fill with orange juice.

Russian Espresso

45 ml vodka
20 ml espresso coffee liqueur
lemon peel

Shake vodka and liqueur well with crushed ice. Strain into a chilled old-fashioned glass and add a twist of lemon.

Screwdriver

45 ml vodka
60 ml orange juice
slice of orange

Pour vodka then juice into an old-fashioned glass with ice cubes and stir. Cut orange slice in half and sit both pieces on rim of glass.

Sea Breeze

45 ml vodka
120 ml cranberry juice
30 ml grapefruit juice
lime wedge

Build the first three ingredients in a highball glass. Garnish with lime wedge.

Sex on the Beach

30 ml vodka
20 ml peach schnapps
cranberry juice
grapefruit juice

Add vodka and schnapps to a highball glass. Fill with equal measures of cranberry juice and grapefruit juice. Stir.

White Russian

30 ml Kahlua
30 ml vodka
30 ml pouring cream

Pour all ingredients into a chilled old-fashioned glass with ice cubes and stir. Serve with a swizzle stick and short straw.

WHISKY

*A distilled spirit made from grain
(barley, rye, oats, etc). It can be
served either straight or blended.
Also 'whiskey', except in Scotland.*

Baby's Bottom

45 ml whisky
15 ml white crème de menthe
15 ml white crème de cacao

Stir all ingredients together in a mixing glass, then strain into a cocktail glass.

Highball

45 ml bourbon
dry ginger ale or soda water
lemon peel

Put a generous number of ice cubes in a highball glass, add the bourbon and top with dry ginger ale or soda. Add a twist of lemon.

Manhattan

20 ml sweet vermouth
75 ml bourbon
dash of angostura bitters
maraschino cherry
orange peel

Combine vermouth, bourbon and bitters in a mixing glass with a few ice cubes. Stir gently (the drink should not go cloudy). Strain mixture over the cherry placed in a chilled cocktail glass. Rub cut edge of orange peel over rim of glass and twist it over the drink.

What whiskey will not cure, there is no cure for.

—IRISH PROVERB

Mint Julep

1 teaspoon castor sugar
4–5 fresh mint leaves (plus an extra sprig)
60 ml bourbon
soda water

Mix mint leaves and sugar in the base of a highball glass to crush sugar and release flavour and aroma of mint. Add bourbon and stir until sugar dissolves. Drop in some ice cubes, top up with soda and add sprig of fresh mint for garnish.

Rusty Nail

30 ml Scotch whisky
40 ml Drambuie
lemon peel (optional)

Pour whisky and Drambuie into an old-fashioned glass and serve on the rocks. Add a twist of lemon if desired.

Seaboard

30 ml whisky
30 ml gin
1 tablespoon lemon juice
1 teaspoon icing sugar
fresh mint leaves

Shake all ingredients (except mint leaves) with ice and strain into an old-fashioned glass over ice cubes. Garnish with mint leaves.

Stiletto

45 ml bourbon
1½ teaspoons amaretto
juice of ½ lemon

Pour all ingredients into an old-fashioned glass over ice cubes and stir.

Tar

45 ml whisky
15 ml dark crème de cacao
½ teaspoon grenadine
juice of lemon

Combine all ingredients in a cocktail shaker with 5 ice cubes, and shake. Pour into a chilled cocktail glass.

WINE

The fermented juice of the grape, in many varieties (red, white, sweet, dry, etc), used as a beverage.

Bordij

60 ml red wine (Bordeaux)
30 ml cognac
20 ml crème de cassis

Combine ingredients and strain into an ice-filled wine glass.

Calimocho

½ glass red wine
½ glass cola

Fill a highball glass with ice, then add the wine and cola.

Champagne Cocktail

sugar cube
dash of angostura bitters
30 ml brandy
champagne
thin orange slice and a strawberry

Place the sugar cube in a champagne saucer and sprinkle with bitters. Add brandy, then top up with champagne. Sit orange on rim of glass and drop strawberry in.

Clove Cocktail

30 ml sweet vermouth
15 ml sloe gin
15 ml muscatel

Stir ingredients with ice and strain into a cocktail glass.

Cocomacoque

45 ml white rum
60 ml orange juice
60 ml pineapple juice
15 ml sour mix
60 ml white wine
spear pineapple

Combine first five ingredients and strain into a highball glass. Garnish with pineapple spear.

From wine what sudden friendship springs!

– JOHN GAY

Drawbridge

150 ml white wine
soda water
dash of blue curaçao

Fill a wine glass with ice and add wine.
Top with soda and a dash of blue curaçao.

Spritzer

60 ml chilled white wine
soda water

Pour ingredients into a chilled wine glass.

Strawberry Kir Royale

2 cups strawberries
1 tablespoon sugar
½ cup champagne
1 teaspoon crème de cassis

Mix strawberries and sugar in a bowl and let stand for 5–10 minutes, stirring occasionally. Divide between two wine glasses and add champagne and crème de cassis. *Serves 2*

PUNCH

A beverage consisting of wine or spirits, mixed with water or fruit juice and flavoured with sugar, lemon, spices, etc. Ideal for large gatherings!

Brunch Punch

3 litres tomato juice, chilled
1 litre rum (dark or light)
150 ml lemon or lime juice
2 teaspoons Worcestershire sauce
salt and freshly ground black pepper
thinly cut lemon or lime slices

Combine all ingredients, stir and pour over a block of ice in a large punch bowl. Garnish with lemon or lime slices.
Serves approximately 40

Egg Nogg

12 eggs
1 cup sugar
1 cup bourbon
1 cup cognac
½ tsp salt
1425 ml heavy cream
freshly grated nutmeg
1–2 cups milk (optional)

Separate eggs and set whites aside. Beat yolks and sugar with electric beater until light in colour, then decrease the speed while adding bourbon and cognac. Refrigerate for 3 hours. Add salt to egg whites, beat into peaks. Whip cream until stiff. Fold whipped cream into yolk mixture, then fold in the beaten whites. Refrigerate for 1 hour. Serve in a punch bowl, with nutmeg sprinkled on top. *Serves 12*

Note: If you prefer a thinner mixture, add 1–2 cups milk

Gluhwein

1 bottle dry red wine
3 tablespoons sugar
2 slices orange
2 slices lemon
freshly grated nutmeg
cinnamon stick
generous dash of brandy (optional)
orange slices studded with cloves

Heat wine, sugar, fruit and spices in a saucepan until hot but not boiling. Stir until the sugar dissolves. Add a dash of brandy if desired. Serve hot in toddy glasses, with a slice of orange in each.
Serves 4

Planter's Punch

60 ml gold or white rum
30 ml lime juice
30 ml orange juice
5 ml sugar syrup
5 ml grenadine
soda water
orange slice

Fill a highball glass two-thirds with ice, then build the first five ingredients into the glass. Fill with soda and stir. Add orange slice and serve with a straw.

Sangria

orange and lemon slices, halved
1 bottle dry red wine (Spanish, if you
    want to be authentic)
60 ml brandy
30 ml curaçao
30 ml orange juice
¼ cup castor sugar

Put ice and fruit slices into a large jug.
Add remaining ingredients and stir well.
Serve in generous-sized wine glasses.
Serves 4

Snake Bite

360 ml lager
300 ml cider
45 ml grenadine

Mix ingredients together in a beer mug.
Serves 1, if you're game!

The best audience is one that is intelligent, well-educated, and a little drunk.

— ALBEN W. BARKLEY

Watermelon Champagne

3 cups cubed, seeded watermelon
1 tablespoon sugar
1 bottle champagne

Place watermelon and sugar in blender and whiz until smooth. Half-fill eight champagne flutes with the watermelon mixture. Slowly fill each flute with champagne. *Serves 8*

NON-ALCOHOLIC

Cocktails without alcohol are often described as 'virgin'. You should always offer non-alcoholic cocktails for those who prefer not to drink alcohol — and for those who do! Stunning drinks do not have to contain alcohol — just try the following...

Apello

40 ml orange juice
30 ml grapefruit juice
10 ml apple juice
maraschino cherry

Stir juices together in an old-fashioned glass, garnish with maraschino cherry.

Cranberry Bomber

120 ml cranberry juice
15 ml orange juice
15 ml grenadine
cola
1 teaspoon honey
lemon slice

Pour first three ingredients into a highball glass over ice and fill with cola. Stir and add honey. Garnish with lemon slice.

Jungle Juice

1 banana
2 cups orange juice
dash of ginger ale

Break banana into chunks and combine with orange juice and ginger ale in blender. Whiz on medium speed until well blended. Pour into highball glasses.
Serves 2

*Though I look old, yet I am strong and lusty
For in my youth I never did apply
Hot and rebellious liquors in my blood.*

— SHAKESPEARE

Mango Lassi

pulp of two ripe mangoes
2 cups yoghurt
½ cup sugar
1 cup iced water

Whiz all ingredients in blender and pour into highball glasses over crushed ice.
Serves 2

Note: Other fruits (strawberries, bananas, etc) can also be used.

Passionfruit Spritzer

120 ml passionfruit juice
soda water
lime wedge

Pour juice into a champagne flute and top up with soda. Garnish with lime wedge.

Safe Sex on the Beach

90 ml cranberry juice
90 ml grapefruit juice
60 ml peach nectar
maraschino cherry

Pour juices and nectar over ice in a chilled highball glass and stir. Garnish with cherry.

Virgin Lime Rickey

30 ml lime juice
soda water
dash of grenadine

Pour lime juice into an old-fashioned glass two-thirds filled with ice. Fill with soda and stir. Add grenadine and stir again.

Hot Toddy

*A drink made of spirits and hot milk
or water, sweetened and sometimes
spiced with cloves.*

After-Dinner Mint

20 ml white crème de menthe
30 ml Southern Comfort
15 ml vodka
150 ml hot chocolate
whipped cream (optional)

Combine crème de menthe, Southern Comfort and vodka in a toddy glass. Add hot chocolate. Garnish with whipped cream if desired.

Amaretto Tea

180 ml hot tea, freshly brewed
60 ml amaretto
whipped cream

Pour hot tea into a pousse-café glass, leaving a spoon in glass to prevent cracking. Add amaretto, but do not stir. Top with whipped cream and serve.

Blueberry Tea

30 ml amaretto
15 ml Grand Marnier
125 ml herbal blueberry tea, freshly brewed

Pour amaretto and Grand Marnier into a brandy snifter and add hot tea.

Hot Buttered Rum

1 teaspoon brown sugar
pinch of nutmeg
cinnamon stick
60 ml boiling water
60 ml dark rum
1 teaspoon butter

Put sugar and spices in a warmed toddy glass. Add boiling water and stir to dissolve sugar. Add rum, then float butter on top. Serve with cinnamon stick.
Note: This should be drunk warm, while the butter melts.

As a cure for the cold, take your toddy to bed, put one bowler hat at the foot, and drink until you see two.

— SIR ROBERT BRUCE LOCKHART

Hot Vanilla

420 ml milk
60 ml whipping cream
½ ground vanilla bean
1½ teaspoons sugar
ground cinnamon

Combine first four ingredients in a heavy saucepan and warm over low heat. When small bubbles appear around sides of pan, remove from heat and let mixture sit at room temperature for 15–20 minutes. Place pan back on stove and rewarm mixture, whisking it briefly to redistribute the skin that forms on the milk's surface. Remove vanilla bean, scrape out seeds with a sharp knife, and return seeds to milk. Pour the vanilla milk into toddy glasses, sprinkle with cinnamon and drink hot. *Serves 2*

Hot Whisky

*60 ml Scotch whisky (or another spirit of
   your choice)*
1 teaspoon honey
boiling water
lemon slice

Pour whisky and honey into a toddy glass,
fill with boiling water and stir to mix.
Float the lemon slice and drink warm.

Jamaican Coffee

60 ml brandy
60 ml white rum
250 ml hot coffee, freshly brewed
freshly grated nutmeg

Divide brandy and rum between two toddy glasses. Fill glasses with hot coffee, sprinkle with nutmeg and drink hot.
Serves 2

Masala Chai

1½ cups water
cinnamon stick
8 cardamom pods
8 cloves
⅔ cup milk
sugar
3 teaspoons tea leaves

Combine water, cinnamon stick, cardamom pods and cloves in a saucepan. When boiling, turn heat to low, cover, and simmer for 10 minutes. Add milk and sugar and bring to simmer again. Throw in tea leaves, cover, and turn off heat. Sit for 2 minutes, then strain tea into toddy glasses. *Serves 2*

MORNING AFTER

If you have over-indulged, the morning after can be a headache, to say the least. Everyone has their own recommendation and we've included a few. But our best advice is to remember that cocktails can be potent and should be consumed in moderation.

Bloody Mary

45 ml vodka
90 ml tomato juice
juice of ½ lemon
few dashes each of Tabasco and
  Worcestershire sauces
slice of lemon
salt and freshly ground black pepper
  (optional)

Combine vodka, juices and sauces with ice. Shake well and strain into a chilled highball glass with ice. Garnish with lemon, and season with salt and pepper if desired.

Bullshot

90 ml vodka
120 ml strong, cold beef bouillon
salt and freshly ground black pepper

Combine vodka and beef boullion with four ice cubes in a mixing glass. Add salt and pepper to taste, stir, and strain into a chilled wine glass.

A hangover is something to fill a head that was empty the night before.

— ANON

Prairie Hen

5 ml vinegar
10 ml Worcestershire sauce
2 dashes of Tabasco sauce
1 egg (do not break yolk)
salt and freshly ground black
  pepper (optional)

Pour ingredients into an old-fashioned glass, season with salt and pepper if desired, and drink (preferably with your eyes closed).

Virgin Mary

120 ml tomato juice
dash of lemon juice
few dashes each of Tabasco and
  Worcestershire sauces
lime wedge

Fill a highball glass with ice. Add tomato juice, then lemon juice and sauces. Stir and garnish with lime wedge.

Glasses

beer mug Up to 700 ml. A thick glass with a handle, the traditional beer container.

brandy snifter Up to 450 ml. A generous-sized, balloon-shaped glass that concentrates the alcoholic odours to the top of the glass as you cradle the drink in your hands.

champagne flute About 150 ml. Perfect for simple but sophisticated cocktails, especially those using wine or champagne.

champagne saucer About 140 ml. Beautifully shaped, for wine or champagne cocktails, or other creamy, frothy short drinks.

Collins Up to 400 ml. Like a highball glass, only taller. Commonly used for soft drinks and alcoholic juices such as the Mai Tai.

cocktail About 90 ml. The classic Martini glass, triangular in shape, usually used for short, strong drinks and aperitifs. The stem ensures your hand doesn't warm the drink.

highball 200–285 ml. A tall, straight-sided glass for long, cool drinks as well as soft drinks, and beer if you don't have beer mugs.

liqueur 30–60 ml. A small-stemmed glass for serving rich liqueurs.

old-fashioned 120–125 ml. A short, businesslike glass for drinks served 'on the rocks', and sometimes whisky or fruit juice.

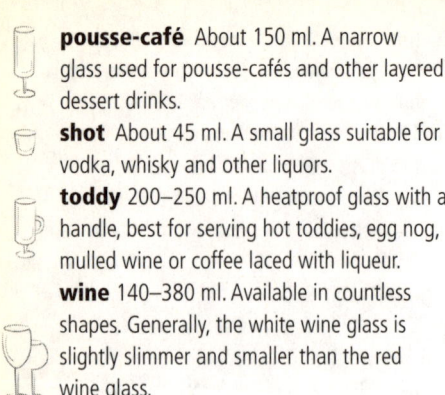

pousse-café About 150 ml. A narrow glass used for pousse-cafés and other layered dessert drinks.

shot About 45 ml. A small glass suitable for vodka, whisky and other liquors.

toddy 200–250 ml. A heatproof glass with a handle, best for serving hot toddies, egg nog, mulled wine or coffee laced with liqueur.

wine 140–380 ml. Available in countless shapes. Generally, the white wine glass is slightly slimmer and smaller than the red wine glass.

GLOSSARY

advocaat A rich, creamy, golden-coloured Dutch liqueur made from eggs, sugar and brandy.

amaretto An amber-coloured Italian liqueur with a nutty apricot flavour.

angostura bitters An aromatic tonic from Trinidad made from a secret blend of herbs and spices.

Bailey's Irish Cream An Irish liqueur of chocolate-flavoured whisky and double cream.

blender If your electric blender does not have specially strengthened blades, use crushed ice, not cubes.

bouillon A plain unclarified stock or broth.

bourbon American whisky, distilled from corn or maize and first produced in Bourbon County, Kentucky. It lacks the subtlety of Scotch whisky, but is a good mixer.

build In a cocktail recipe, this means to pour the ingredients directly into the glass, one on top of the other. Do not stir.

cachaça A Brazilian liquor distilled from sugarcane juice.

champagne A sparkling white wine produced in the wine region of Champagne, France (or, unofficially, a similar wine produced elsewhere).

Chartreuse A French liqueur, made from over 130 herbs and spices. Green Chartreuse is the most common variety, though a yellow version is also available.

cherry brandy Really a cherry liqueur, produced by macerating fruit in a brandy base.

cider The pressed juice of apples drunk either before fermentation (sweet cider) or after fermentation (rough cider).

coffee liqueur A spirit-based liqueur flavoured with coffee.

cognac The smooth, fine, aged brandy from the French Cognac region. The initials VSOP on the label stand for 'Very Special Old Pale'.

Cointreau A colourless, orange-flavoured French liqueur, like a very fine curaçao.

crème de These words usually indicate a sweet brandy-based liqueur, though not necessarily with a creamy flavour or appearance.

crème de banane A pungent, brandy-based banana liqueur.

crème de cacao A dark brown or white (clear) chocolate-flavoured liqueur made from the cacao seed.

crème de cassis A dark, syrupy blackcurrant liqueur.

crème de framboise A delicately flavoured raspberry liqueur.

crème de menthe A sweet, green or white (clear) liqueur with a strong mint flavour.

crème de noyeaux An almond-flavoured French liqueur.

crème de violette A fragrant liqueur with the exotic flavour and colour of violets.
curaçao A sweet, orange-flavoured liqueur which comes in orange, white (clear), green, red and blue (although the flavour remains basically the same).
Drambuie A whisky liqueur made from Scotch malt whisky and heather honey.
Frangelico An Italian hazelnut-flavoured liqueur named after a legendary liqueur-making hermit.
frost To coat the rim of a glass with salt or sugar, depending on whether the drink is sweet or not. To do this, hold the glass (a cocktail glass works best) by the stem and dip it into lemon juice or rub a piece of lemon

around the rim. Spread the salt or sugar evenly on a small plate and dip the rim in, giving the glass a small twist.

Grand Marnier An orange-flavoured French cognac liqueur, first made in the 1880s.

grenadine A non-alcoholic sugar syrup, pink in colour, flavoured with pomegranate.

Kahlua A Mexican liqueur flavoured with coffee beans and brandy.

lager A type of German beer brewed by the slow fermentation of yeast at low temperatures.

madeira A fortified wine, originally produced on the island of Madeira.

Malibu A sweet, coconut-flavoured white rum.

maraschino A colourless Italian cherry

liqueur made from marasca cherries and their kernels. It has a delicate, nutty flavour.

maraschino cherries These come in a range of colours (even blue!) and are used as a garnish. They can float on top of a cocktail, rest on the rim of the glass or be speared, singly or in clusters, on a toothpick and balanced across the glass. Alternatively, fresh cherries can be hung over the rim of the glass.

muscatel Wine made from sweet, aromatic 'muscat' grapes.

on the rocks Poured over ice cubes.

orgeat A non-alcoholic, sweetened syrup, flavoured with almond, rose and orange blossom.

ouzo A Greek aniseed-flavoured spirit which

is clear in colour but turns milky when water is added.

peach nectar A mixture of peach juice, peach puree, sugar and water. Available in supermarkets.

sake A Japanese fermented alcoholic drink made from rice.

sambuca A clear Roman liqueur with the flavours of elderbrush and licorice.

schnapps A gin-based liqueur, often flavoured with caraway or cumin.

Scotch whisky Any whisky distilled in Scotland, but usually a blended whisky.

shaker The classic cocktail shaker comes in three pieces, with a strainer in the top. Most are stainless steel or silver. Never fill your shaker to the top and always make sure it is securely closed.

sloe gin A red-coloured liqueur made from sloes (a type of berry) macerated in gin.

sour mix Also known as 'sweet and sour mix' or 'bar mix', this is a mixer made of lemon or lime juice and sugar syrup. It is available at most liquor stores but to make your own, mix one part heavy sugar syrup (3 parts sugar, 2 parts water) with one part lemon juice. To make drinks slightly foamy, add 2 egg whites per litre of mix. Adjust the sugar/juice ratio to give the mix the right balance of sweetness and tartness.

Southern Comfort An American liqueur, combining bourbon whisky with peaches and a faint trace of orange. More like a spirit than a liqueur, it is comparatively dry and potent.

strainer To strain cocktails, use either the classic 'Hawthorne' strainer or one of the practical clip-on varieties.

sugar syrup A solution of sugar and water (heated over a low flame until clear, then briefly boiled). It can be made in various densities – 2 parts water to 1 part sugar for a light syrup, and 1 part sugar to one part water (or even 3 parts sugar to 2 parts water) for a heavy syryp.

Tabasco sauce A fiery sauce, prepared from the fruit of a variety of capsicum, salt and distilled natural vinegar.

triple sec A dry, colourless, highly refined curaçao.

twist When a recipe asks for a 'twist' of lemon or lime, hold a piece of peel over the drink and twist gently to release a few drops of natural oil. This adds a subtle flavour and aroma to the drink. It is usual to then drop the peel into the cocktail.

vermouth A fortified, aromatic wine made in France and Italy. Usually served as an aperitif, it is available in dry, sweet (rosso) and medium-sweet (bianco).

Worcestershire sauce A sharp sauce made with soya sauce, vinegar, spices, etc.

I never have more than one drink before dinner. But I do like that one to be large and very strong and very cold and very well made.

— JAMES BOND